THIS BOOK BELONGS TO...

Name: | Age:

Favourite player:

2018/2019

WITHDRAWN FROM STOCK

	My Predictions...	Actual...
The Rams' final position:		
The Rams' top scorer:		
Championship Winners:		
Championship top scorer:		
FA Cup Winners:		
EFL Cup Winners:		

Contributors: Peter Rogers

A TWOCAN PUBLICATION

©2018. Published by twocan under licence from Derby County Football Club.

ISBN 978-1-912692-32-3

PICTURE CREDITS: Action Images, Andy Clarke, Derby County Football Club, Press Association.

£9

CONTENTS

1 SCOTT CARSON

GOALKEEPER **DOB: 03/09/85** **COUNTRY: ENGLAND**

The Rams' No.1 Scott Carson went into the 2018/19 campaign off the back of what was arguably the best season of his career so far. Numerous landmarks were passed, as he kept his 50th clean sheet in a Derby shirt, as well as recording 20 shutouts in a single season for the first time in a career that has spanned nearly 15 years.

2 ANDRE WISDOM

DEFENDER **DOB: 09/05/93** **COUNTRY: ENGLAND**

After leaving a lasting impression when he starred on loan from Liverpool during the 2013/14 season, Andre arrived at Pride Park Stadium in the summer of 2017 and picked up where he left off by helping Derby to another Play-Off campaign last term. Wisdom also has international experience, having represented England at U16, U17, U19 and U21 level.

SQUAD 2018/19

3 CRAIG FORSYTH

DEFENDER **DOB:** 24/02/89 **COUNTRY:** SCOTLAND

After two injury-disrupted campaigns, Craig returned to regular action with the Rams during the 2017/18 season. The Scottish international defender's versatility makes him a key player, as he is able to switch from his regular left-back position into a left-sided central-defensive role.

4 CRAIG BRYSON

MIDFIELDER **DOB:** 06/11/86 **COUNTRY:** SCOTLAND

2017/18 was a season of change for Craig, as the midfielder spent time away from Pride Park Stadium with Neil Warnock's Cardiff City, and the midfielder scored twice in 22 appearances as the Welsh club secured their return to the Premier League. One of Bryson's biggest highlights in a Derby shirt came in 2014 when he netted a memorable hat-trick in the 5-0 demolition of arch-rivals Nottingham Forest.

5 FIKAYO **TOMORI**

DEFENDER **DOB:** 19/12/97 **COUNTRY:** ENGLAND

Fikayo joined the Rams on a season-long loan in August 2018 from Chelsea and made his debut against Leeds United. Tomori was part of the England U20 team that were victorious in the 2017 FIFA U20 World Cup, beating Venezuela in the final 1–0.

6 RICHARD **KEOGH**

DEFENDER **DOB:** 11/08/86 **COUNTRY:** REPUBLIC OF IRELAND

At the start of this season, Richard was closing in on 300 games for the Rams. The Republic of Ireland international's consistency, determination and character played a key role in the 20 clean sheets that Derby kept across the 48-game league campaign last time around. Keogh was part of Martin O'Neill's squad for UEFA Euro 2016 and he featured in the Green Army's historic 1-0 win over Italy, before starting against host nation France in the last-16 of the competition.

7 HARRY WILSON

MIDFIELDER   **DOB: 22/03/97**   **COUNTRY: WALES**

Harry arrived at Pride Park in the summer of 2018 from Premier League Liverpool on a season-long loan. Wilson became the youngest-ever player to represent Wales when he made his debut against Belgium at the age of 16 years and 207 days and earlier this year, he scored his first goal for Wales in a 6-0 win against china on his 21st birthday.

SQUAD 2018/19

8 MASON MOUNT

MIDFIELDER   **DOB: 10/01/99**   **COUNTRY: ENGLAND**

An exciting prospect, 19-year-old Mason joined the Rams on a season-long loan from Chelsea during the summer and scored on his Derby debut in the first game of the season, away at Reading. Last season, he had a very successful loan spell with Vitesse, scoring 14 goals in 39 appearances in all competitions. He has also represented England at U16, U17, U18 and U19 level.

9 MARTYN WAGHORN

FORWARD   **DOB: 23/01/90**   **COUNTRY: ENGLAND**

Martyn began his career at Sunderland at the age of eight and made his first-team debut for the club in December 2007 against Manchester United, at the age of 17. He arrived at Pride Park during the summer from Ipswich Town, where he was top scorer last term with 16 goals. He scored his first league goal in Derby colours in a 2-1 win at Hull City from the penalty spot in September 2018.

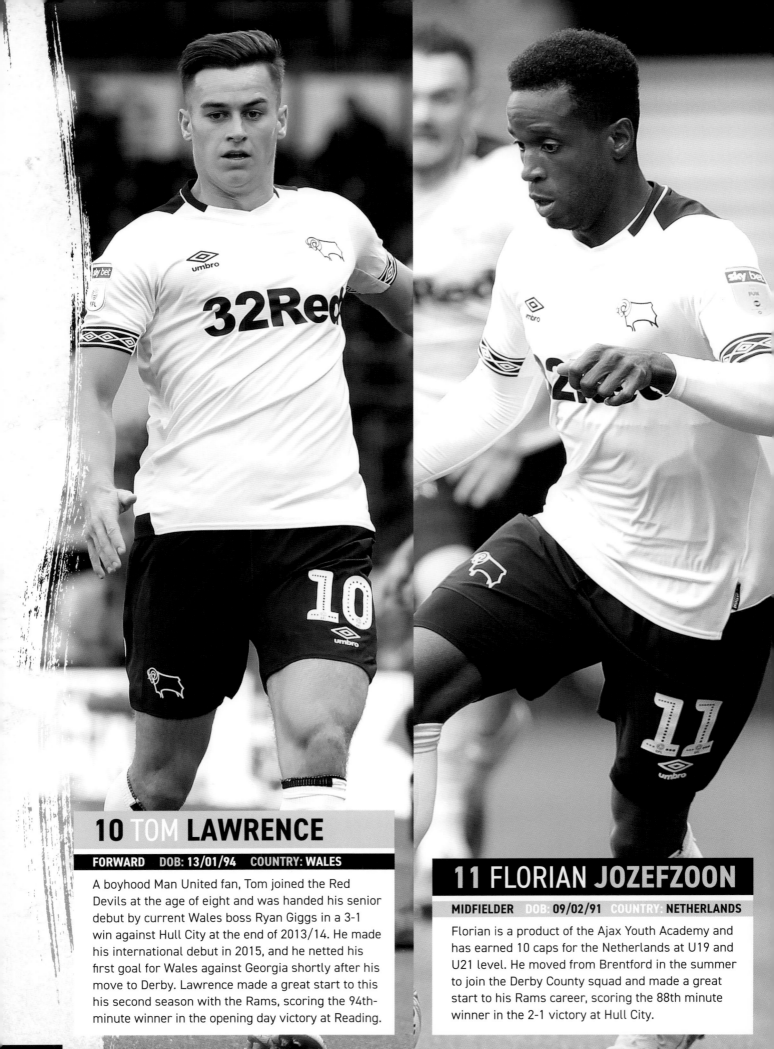

10 TOM LAWRENCE

FORWARD   **DOB: 13/01/94**   **COUNTRY: WALES**

A boyhood Man United fan, Tom joined the Red Devils at the age of eight and was handed his senior debut by current Wales boss Ryan Giggs in a 3-1 win against Hull City at the end of 2013/14. He made his international debut in 2015, and he netted his first goal for Wales against Georgia shortly after his move to Derby. Lawrence made a great start to this his second season with the Rams, scoring the 94th-minute winner in the opening day victory at Reading.

11 FLORIAN JOZEFZOON

MIDFIELDER   **DOB: 09/02/91**   **COUNTRY: NETHERLANDS**

Florian is a product of the Ajax Youth Academy and has earned 10 caps for the Netherlands at U19 and U21 level. He moved from Brentford in the summer to join the Derby County squad and made a great start to his Rams career, scoring the 88th minute winner in the 2-1 victory at Hull City.

15 BRADLEY **JOHNSON**

MIDFIELDER   **DOB: 28/04/87**   **COUNTRY: ENGLAND**

Bradley signed for Derby on transfer deadline day on 1 September 2015. Now in his fourth season with the Rams, his experience and quality in midfield remain a vital asset. Johnson appeared in central-midfield, out wide and in the No.10 role during the course of last season, and his versatility is will be vital in Derby's push for promotion.

14 JACK **MARRIOTT**

FORWARD   **DOB: 09/09/94**   **COUNTRY: ENGLAND**

The Rams signed Peterborough United striker Jack in July 2018 after the 23-year-old had scored 27 goals in League One for the Posh last season. The striker's first appearance in a Derby shirt came in 2-0 EFL Cup with against Oldham Athletic at Boundary Park.

SQUAD 2018/19

16 ALEX **PEARCE**

DEFENDER   **DOB: 09/11/88**   **COUNTRY: REPUBLIC OF IRELAND**

Alex progressed through the youth system at Reading and enjoyed nine years at the Madejski Stadium, helping them win promotion to the Premier League in 2012, before joining the Rams in 2015. He has nine caps for the Republic of Ireland and marked his debut in style by scoring in a 4-1 victory over Oman.

32Red

17 GEORGE EVANS

MIDFIELDER   DOB: 13/12/94   COUNTRY: ENGLAND

George signed for Manchester city as a six-year-old and was at their Academy during manager Frank Lampard's time at the club. Evans, who joined the Rams' set up from Reading in the summer, is most comfortable in a defensive midfield role, but has also been known to slot in as centre-back.

18 JACOB BUTTERFIELD

MIDFIELDER   10/06/90   ENGLAND

Jacob, a former Manchester United youngster, quickly burst onto the scene with Barnsley. He made exactly 100 appearances for the Reds between 2007 and 2012 and, at the age of 21, he captained the side. Jacob spent the 2017/18 season on loan at Sheffield Wednesday and he went on to play 23 times for the Owls.

20 MASON BENNETT

FORWARD   **DOB: 15/07/96**   **COUNTRY: ENGLAND**

At just 15 years and 99 days old, Mason became Derby's youngest-ever player when he was named in the starting line-up in a 2-0 defeat at Middlesbrough in October 2011. He hit the crossbar at the Riverside Stadium and impressed with a lively display in attack. He has also represented England at U16, U17 and U19 level.

21 KELLE ROOS

GOALKEEPER   **DOB: 31/05/92**   **COUNTRY: NETHERLANDS**

Kelle started the 2017/18 campaign in Sky Bet League Two with Port Vale, but he was soon playing a key role as Plymouth Argyle surged up the League One table. The former Dutch youth international joined the Pilgrims on loan amidst a goalkeeping crisis, and he repaid the faith by going unbeaten in each of his four appearances

SQUAD 2018/19

23 DUANE HOLMES

MIDFIELDER **DOB: 06/11/94** **COUNTRY: USA**

Duane was born in the USA, but moved to England at a young age. He joined Huddersfield Town as an U9 and progressed to their first team before moving to Scunthorpe United in 2016, where last season he netted nine goals in 54 games. Blessed with skill and pace, the 23-year-old snapped up five awards at The Iron's end-of-season awards, including Fans' Player of the Year and Players' Player of the Year.

29 MARCUS OLSSON

DEFENDER **DOB: 17/05/88** **COUNTRY: SWEDEN**

Marcus suffered a cruel end to his 2017/18 campaign, as a serious knee injury suffered against Barnsley on the final day ruled him out of the Play-Off showdown with Fulham. He will be fighting hard to return to the squad at some point during the 2018/19 season and put his top-flight and international experience to good use.

28 DAVID NUGENT

FORWARD **DOB: 02/05/85** **COUNTRY: ENGLAND**

David adds a unique attacking threat as well as crucial experience to Derby's cause and with nine goals in all competitions last season, he was the Rams' second highest scorer. He also has 14 England U21 caps to his name and he has a one cap, one goal record at senior level, after scoring for England in a 3-0 Euro 2008 qualifying victory against Andorra.

30 IKECHI ANYA

MIDFIELDER **DOB: 03/01/88** **COUNTRY: SCOTLAND**

After appearing against Wolves as a substitute in August 2017, Ikechi had to wait until January for his next appearance, where he had a late goal wrongly disallowed for offside against Millwall. He featured regularly during the latter part of the campaign, including the Play-Off semi-final second leg against Fulham. He has played 29 times for Scotland since making his debut in 2013 and has scored three goals.

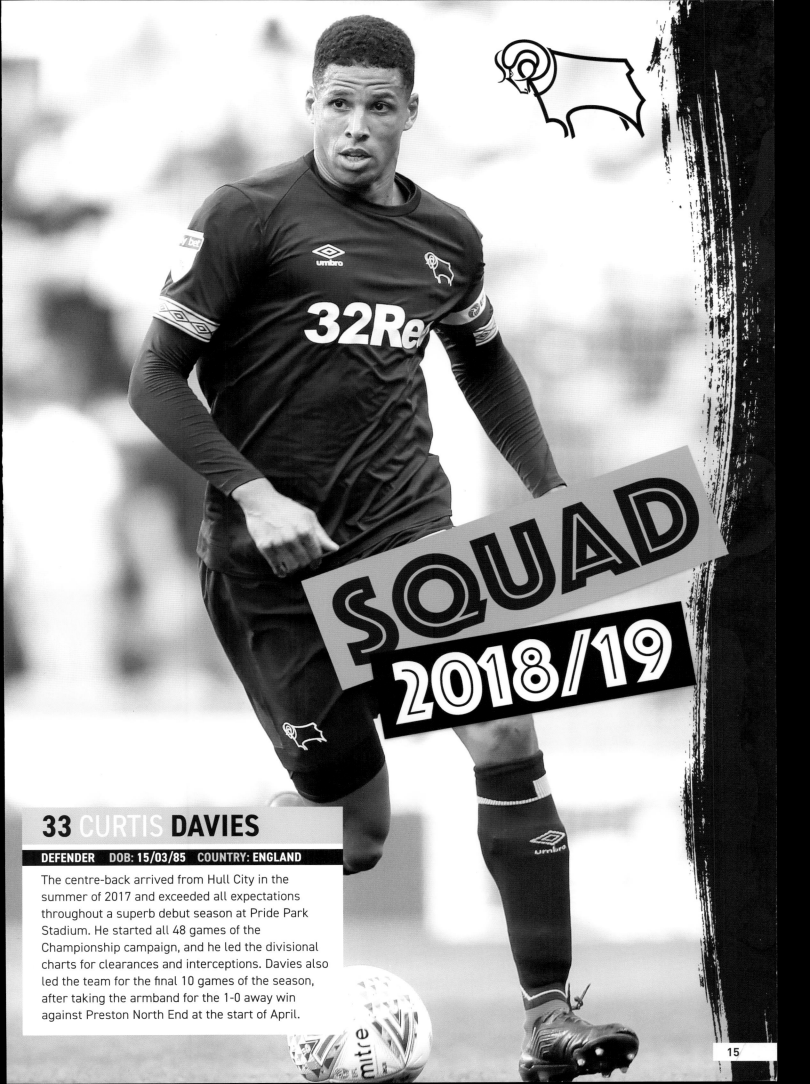

SQUAD 2018/19

33 CURTIS DAVIES

DEFENDER   DOB: 15/03/85   COUNTRY: ENGLAND

The centre-back arrived from Hull City in the summer of 2017 and exceeded all expectations throughout a superb debut season at Pride Park Stadium. He started all 48 games of the Championship campaign, and he led the divisional charts for clearances and interceptions. Davies also led the team for the final 10 games of the season, after taking the armband for the 1-0 away win against Preston North End at the start of April.

34 GEORGE THORNE

MIDFIELDER   DOB: 04/01/93   COUNTRY: ENGLAND

George was a graduate of West Bromwich Albion's Academy and made his first-team debut at only16 years of age during 2009/10. Thorne became an instant hit at Derby during a twelve-game loan spell in the second half of the 2013/14 campaign as he helped the club reach the Play-Off Final. In July 2014 the club signed Thorne on a permanent basis.

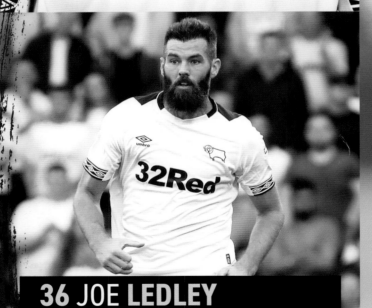

36 JOE LEDLEY

MIDFIELDER   DOB: 23/01/87   COUNTRY: WALES

Ledley started out at his hometown club, Cardiff City, where he amassed over 200 appearances and was an instrumental figure in the club reaching the FA Cup Final in 2008 and Championship Play-Off Final two years later. After spells at Celtic and Crystal Palace, Joe's career led him to Pride Park in 2017. He has also made over 75 appearances for his country and played in all of Wales' games at the UEFA Euro 2016 Finals.

37 JAYDEN BOGLE

DEFENDER   DOB: 27/07/00   COUNTRY: ENGLAND

After excelling for the U18s, Jayden Bogle's name was added to the 2018/19 first team squad list. He made his debut in a first round EFL Cup 2–0 win at Oldham Athletic on 14th August and four days later made his Championship bow at Millwall, earning great praise from Manager Frank Lampard.

44 TOM HUDDLESTONE

MIDFIELDER **DOB: 28/12/86** **COUNTRY: ENGLAND**

Tom started out with spells in Nottingham Forest's and Derby County's youth ranks before signing a Pro contract with the Rams. He was a regular over his first two years at Pride Park Stadium and made 95 appearances, before moving to Tottenham Hotspur. After a successful eight-year stay in the capital and by way of Hull City, Tom's career turned full circle returning to his boyhood club in the summer of 2017.

46 SCOTT MALONE

DEFENDER **DOB: 25/03/91** **COUNTRY: ENGLAND**

Scott joined the Wolverhampton Wanderers' Academy at the age of nine and was voted their Academy Player of the Season in 2008/09. The left-sided defender made the move to Pride Park Stadium in the summer of 2018 from Premier League Huddersfield Town.

FIKAYO TOMORI

Magic MOMENT

66'

Derby County reached the Premier League promised land following a vital 2-1 victory over Crystal Palace in their final home game of the 1995/96 season.

Jim Smith's Rams went into the Palace fixture knowing that victory would send them up. Derby enjoyed the perfect start as Dean Sturridge scored inside two and a half minutes. Palace quickly equalised through Kenny Brown as the first-half ended 1-1.

Robin Van der Laan then became the toast of the Baseball Ground as he headed the Rams back in front after 66 minutes.

The result saw Derby seal second spot behind champions Sunderland, while Palace were left to face the Play-Offs.

GOING *Up!*

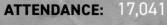

FIXTURE:	Endsleigh League Division One
DATE:	Sunday 28 April 1996
SCORE:	Derby County 2 Crystal Palace 1
VENUE:	Baseball Ground
ATTENDANCE:	17,041

DANGER MEN

Watch out for these Danger Men when the Rams meet their Championship rivals...

ASTON VILLA
Jack Grealish

Attacking midfielder Jack Grealish is sure to be the driving force behind Aston Villa once again in 2018/19.

The talented playmaker is a Villa fan and will be going full throttle to help Steve Bruce's side win promotion back to the Premier League. Villa were delighted to keep him at the club following a summer of speculation about the England under-21 star's future.

BOLTON WANDERERS
Yanic Wildschut

Dutch midfielder Yanic Wildschut joined Bolton Wanderers on a season-long loan deal from Championship rivals Norwich City in July 2018.

The talented 27-year-old, who loves to run at the opposition, enjoyed the perfect start to his Bolton career by scoring the winning goal on the opening day of the season away to West Bromwich Albion.

BIRMINGHAM CITY
Che Adams

After joining Blues from Sheffield United in August 2016, all-action midfielder Che Adams wasted little time in showing the St Andrew's faithful just what he was all about.

Adams wrote his name into Birmingham City folklore on the final day of the 2016/17 campaign, scoring the goal that preserved the club's Championship status. He is sure to be a key player for Garry Monk's men in 2018-19.

BRENTFORD
Ollie Watkins

One of the most exciting and talented footballers outside of the Premier League, Ollie Watkins has been a roaring success since joining Brentford from Exeter City in the summer of 2017.

He netted an impressive eleven goals in all competitions in his first season at Griffin Park. He loves to let fly from distance and has scored a number of spectacular goals for the Bees.

BLACKBURN ROVERS
Elliott Bennett

Experienced winger Elliott Bennett played a vital role in Rovers' promotion from League One in 2017/18.

The former Brighton and Norwich man has been a great influence on the younger players at Ewood Park and will be an important member of Tony Mowbray's team once again now they are back in the Championship.

BRISTOL CITY
Andreas Weimann

Much-travelled Austrian striker Andreas Weimann joined Bristol City ahead of the 2018/19 season, agreeing a three-year deal at Ashton Gate.

Weimann is a vastly experienced forward who knows the English game well following spells with Aston Villa, Watford, Derby County and Wolves. The Robins will be looking for Weimann to grab the goals to fire them into Play-Off contention.

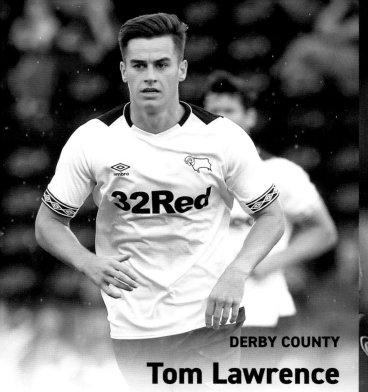

DERBY COUNTY
Tom Lawrence

Wales international midfielder Tom Lawrence, looks set to play a vital role at Pride Park in 2018/19 under new Derby boss Frank Lampard.

The Rams' midfielder certainly has an eye for goal and with Lampard to guide him, Lawrence could well become one of the Championship's star turns over the coming months. He began the season in fine form with two goals in Derby's opening two games.

LEEDS UNITED
Patrick Bamford

A proven goalscorer in the Championship, Patrick Bamford joined Leeds United in the summer of 2018 from Middlesbrough.

Bamford is a great finisher, who also has great awareness of those around him. His arrival at Elland Road has certainly heightened the levels of expectation among the Leeds United fans.

HULL CITY
Fraizer Campbell

Vastly-experienced striker Fraizer Campbell brings an enormous amount of knowhow to the Tigers' front line.

A former England international, Campbell has spent time on the books at some of the country's biggest clubs including Manchester United and Tottenham Hotspur. Now in his second spell with Hull, he was on target against Sheffield Wednesday to ensure the Tigers' first point of the 2018/19 season.

MIDDLESBROUGH
Britt Assombalonga

Former Nottingham Forest striker Britt Assombalonga joined Middlesbrough in July 2015 for a club record fee of £15M.

He was a consistent goalscorer with both Peterborough United and Forest. Assombalonga netted 13 goals as Boro reached the Play-Off semi-finals last season. Boro will be looking for him to be heavily among the goals again in 2018/19 as they look to mount a successful promotion bid.

IPSWICH TOWN
Jon Nolan

Talented midfielder Jon Nolan was an instrumental player for Shrewsbury Town in 2017/18 as the Shrews reached both the Checkatrade Trophy final and the League One Play-Off final.

In August 2018, he joined Ipswich Town and reunited with his former Shrewsbury boss Paul Hurst who took over at Portman Road three months earlier. Nolan is expected to flourish at Championship level.

MILLWALL
Steve Morison

Evergreen forward Steve Morison is currently enjoying his second spell with the Lions.

His goals helped propel the South London club to the verge of the Play-Offs last season. Approaching 300 games for Millwall and almost 100 goals, Morison is a vital member of Neil Harris' squad with a positive influence both on and off the pitch.

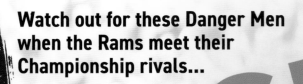

DANGER MEN

Watch out for these Danger Men when the Rams meet their Championship rivals...

NORWICH CITY
Jordan Rhodes

Signed on loan from Sheffield Wednesday, the Canaries will be hopeful that striker Jordan Rhodes can rediscover his goalscoring form during the 2018/19 season at Carrow Road.

A prolific marksman with Huddersfield Town and Blackburn Rovers, Rhodes marked his Carrow Road debut with a goal during a thrilling seven-goal clash with West Bromwich Albion.

QUEENS PARK RANGERS
Eberechi Eze

After spending a loan spell with Wycombe Wanderers last season, Eze has returned to Loftus Road and cemented himself a place in the heart of the Hoops' midfield.

A true box-to-box midfielder, Eze loves to plough forward and lend his support to attacking situations. The 20-year-old produced a number of eye-catching displays at the start of the 2018/19 season and was on target in Rangers' first home game of the season against Sheffield United.

NOTTINGHAM FOREST
Lewis Grabban

A proven Championship goalscorer, Lewis Grabban joined Nottingham Forest in July 2018 for a fee believed to have been in the region of £6M.

His arrival at the City Ground is expected to relieve some of the pressure for goals on fellow frontman Daryl Murphy. Grabban has played for a host of clubs and appears to have the handy knack of always taking his scoring boots with him.

READING
Jon Dadi Bodvarsson

Icelandic international forward Jon Dadi Bodvarsson has become something of a cult hero with Reading fans at the Madejski Stadium after netting ten goals for the Royals last season.

He represented his country at the 2018 World Cup finals in Russia and also netted Reading's first goal of the new 2018/19 campaign.

PRESTON NORTH END
Tom Barkhuizen

After beginning his career with Preston's rivals Blackpool, striker Tom Barkhuizen is a player who will be looking to make his mark for Alex Neil's side in 2018/19.

A string of loan spells with Hereford United, Fleetwood Town and Morecambe resulted in a permanent switch to Morecambe and it was his goalscoring form at the Globe Arena that alerted North End who signed him in November 2016.

ROTHERHAM UNITED
Joe Newell

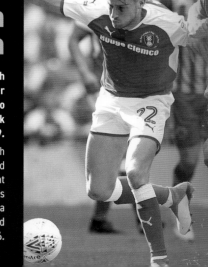

Versatile midfielder Joe Newell was one of the Millers' heroes as Rotherham United won promotion to the Championship via the League One Play-Offs.

With the ability to operate in a creative central midfield berth or out on the wing, Newell was almost ever-present for the Millers last season and will be a key performer for Paul Warne's men in their 2018/19 Championship campaign.

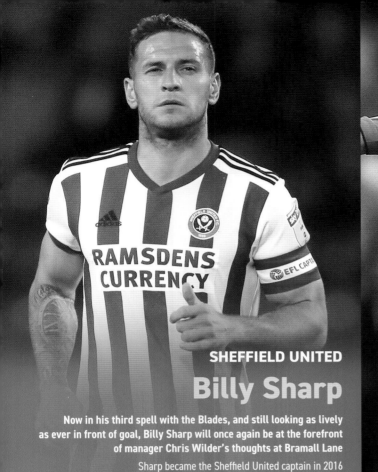

SHEFFIELD UNITED
Billy Sharp

Now in his third spell with the Blades, and still looking as lively as ever in front of goal, Billy Sharp will once again be at the forefront of manager Chris Wilder's thoughts at Bramall Lane

Sharp became the Sheffield United captain in 2016 and is now closing in on 200 goals for the club.

SWANSEA CITY
Oliver McBurnie

Following a highly productive loan spell in the Championship with Barnsley in the second-half of last season, Oliver McBurnie has earned the chance to lead the line for Swansea City as the Welsh club bid to bounce back to the top-flight in 2018/19.

McBurnie scored nine goals in 17 outings for a struggling Tykes team last season and will now look to grab his Swansea opportunity with both hands.

SHEFFIELD WEDNESDAY
Fernando Forestieri

The jewel in Sheffield Wednesday's crown, all eyes at Hillsborough will once again be on skilful Italian Fernando Forestieri who is the man that makes the Owls tick.

The Wednesday fans will be looking for Forestieri to inspire those around him as the club searches for an improved season under Jos Luhakay.

WEST BROMWICH ALBION
Jay Rodriguez

Burnley-born England striker Jay Rodriguez began his career at his hometown club before moving on to the Premier League with Southampton and then West Bromwich Albion.

A cool customer with the ball at his feet, Rodriguez has all the skills to really shine in the Championship for an Albion side who will hope their stay in the second-tier is a brief one.

STOKE CITY
Benik Afobe

Striker Benik Afobe is the man charged with scoring the goals to fire Stoke City back to the Premier League at the first time of asking.

Afobe joined the Potters on loan from Wolverhampton Wanderers in June 2018 and his physical presence and goal threat are sure to play a huge part in the Potters' 2018/19 promotion push.

WIGAN ATHLETIC
Nick Powell

Midfielder Nick Powell was nominated for the EFL League One Player of the Season award after an outstanding season in the Latics' 2017/18 title-winning campaign.

A technically gifted player with the ability to score goals and create chances for others, Powell will certainly be one of the first names on Paul Cook's teamsheet as Wigan look to establish themselves at Championship level.

Defender Colin Todd arrived at the Baseball Ground in February 1971 from Sunderland for a then British record transfer fee for a defender of £175,000. He was already well acquainted to working with Rams' boss Brian Clough having been coached by him at youth level while at Roker Park.

Together with central-defensive partner Roy McFarland, the two defenders provided the foundation upon which Clough built the club's 1971/72 First Division championship-winning team.

After winning the title in '71/72, Derby enjoyed a memorable adventure in the European Cup in 1972/73, with Todd shining at both domestic and European level. He was capped by England 27 times during his time at the Baseball Ground.

BORN:

COLIN TODD · 12 DECEMBER 1948
CHESTER-LE-STREET, COUNTY DURHAM

POSITION:

CENTRAL DEFENDER

RAMS DEBUT:

DERBY COUNTY 2 ARSENAL 1
DIVISION ONE · 27 FEBRUARY 1971

PLAYER OF THE SEASON:

1971/72

STAT ATTACK
COLIN TODD

RAMS APPEARANCES:

APPEARANCES	LEAGUE	FA CUP	LEAGUE CUP	OTHERS
371	293	30	20	28

RAMS GOALS:

GOALS	LEAGUE	FA CUP	LEAGUE CUP	OTHERS
10	6	2	1	1

ENGLAND INTERNATIONAL:

APPEARANCES	GOALS
27	0

INTERNATIONAL DEBUT:

ENGLAND 0-1 NORTHERN IRELAND
23 MAY 1972

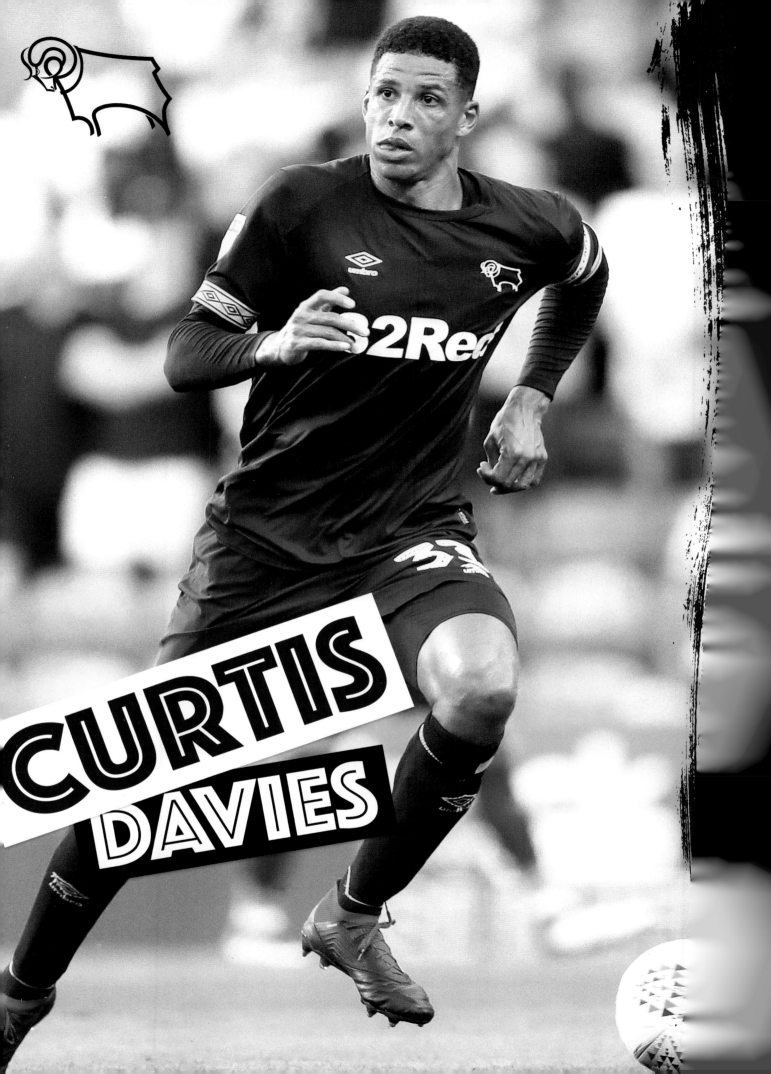

CURTIS
DAVIES

FAN 'TASTIC

There are five England World Cup stars hiding in the crowd... Can you spot them?

ANSWERS ON PAGE 62

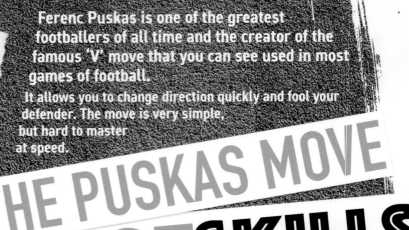

Ferenc Puskas is one of the greatest footballers of all time and the creator of the famous 'V' move that you can see used in most games of football.

It allows you to change direction quickly and fool your defender. The move is very simple, but hard to master at speed.

THE PUSKAS MOVE

#BOY'S GOT SKILLS

TIP:
Use this move when you need to lose your defender. Pretend to strike the ball, your opponent will move to block your faked shot, allowing you to move freely in another direction.

TIP:
Always wait until your defender lunges for the ball before performing the Puskas move.

1. Start by dribbling the ball, keep it as near to your foot as possible while moving forward.

2. Move as if to kick the ball, but rather than striking it, bring your foot over the top of the ball.

TIP:
Don't perform this move too often or your opponents will learn to expect it!

3. Use the bottom of your foot to quickly drag the ball back to you.

4. Now change direction. You can finish the move with a shot at goal or by passing to a teammate.

**Have fun colouring
this picture of Jayden Bogle...**

JAYDEN BOGLE 37

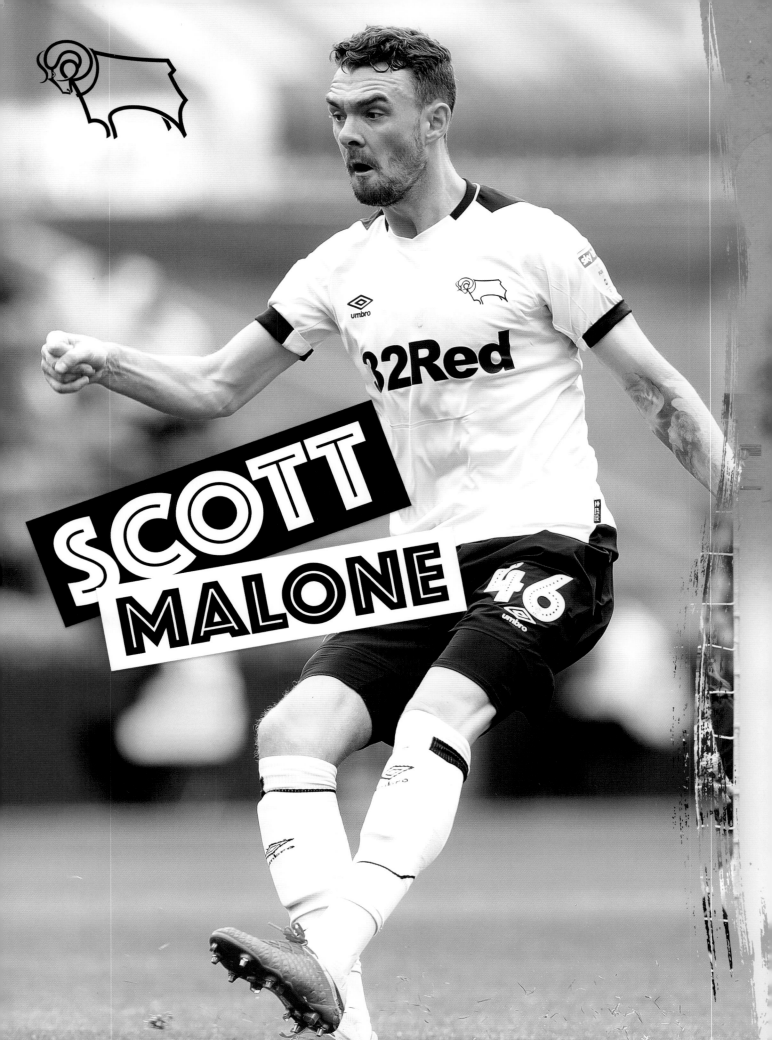

SCOTT MALONE

Magic MOMENT

61'

WEMBLEY *Winners*

FIXTURE: Championship Play-Off final

DATE: Monday 28 May 2007

SCORE: Derby County 1 West Bromwich Albion 0

VENUE: Wembley

ATTENDANCE: 74,993

31 MARTYN

PEARSON 25
McSHANE 20

28 BARNES

BARNES 28

McSHANE 20
PEARSON 25

HOWARD 9

On a rain-soaked afternoon at Wembley, Stephen Pearson was the Rams' goalscoring hero as Billy Davies' team won the 2007 Play-Off final and secured promotion to the Premier League.

After finishing the season in third place in the Championship table, Derby had overcome Southampton in a dramatic semi-final to tee-up a promotion shootout with West Bromwich Albion at Wembley.

Pearson scored the only goal of the game, as he converted Giles Barnes' low cross in the 61st minute. The goal was Pearson's first for the Rams following his move from Celtic four months earlier.

LEDLEY
36

GOALS
GOALS
GO

GUESS THE CLUB

Can you work out which European Club each set of clues is pointing to?

1 ANSWER

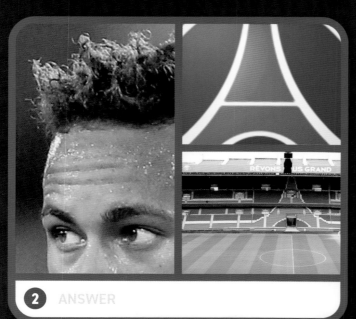

3 ANSWER

2 ANSWER

4 ANSWER

5 ANSWER

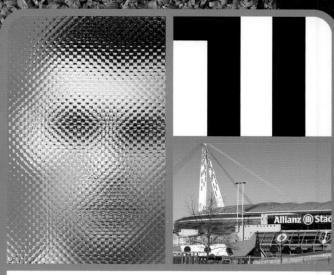

8 ANSWER

6 ANSWER

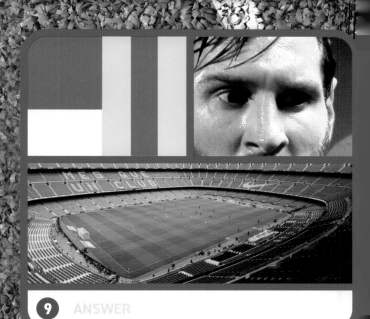

9 ANSWER

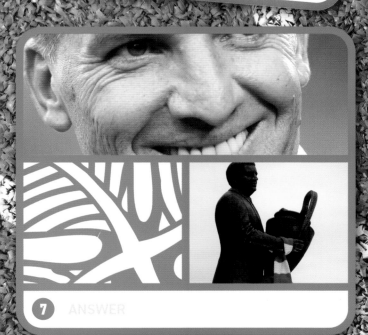

7 ANSWER

10 ANSWER

LOCAL HEROES

Derby County's arch-rivals are Nottingham Forest with both clubs searching for local bragging rights when they go head-to-head in the East Midlands derby matches.

With Forest based at the City Ground, some 14 miles from Pride Park, the geographical rivalry between the two clubs was heightened further in the 1970s after former Derby boss Brian Clough became manager at Forest.

There are seldom better things in life for Derby County fans than watching the Rams defeat Nottingham Forest.

Here are three great derby day triumphs for the Rams from the modern era.

DERBY COUNTY 5
NOTTINGHAM FOREST 0
22 MARCH 2014

After suffering a narrow 1-0 defeat at the City Ground in September 2013, when the two sides met in the first East Midlands derby of the 2013/14 season, the Rams gained sweet revenge by dishing out a real hammering to their rivals in the return fixture.

Craig Bryson turned out to the toast of Derby as he wrote his name into Rams' folklore with a never-to-be-forgotten hat-trick in this five-goal thrashing of Forest.

Saturday 22 March 2014 will go down as one of the greatest days in Derby's recent history as Bryson struck first after six minutes and again after 32. Jeff Hendrick added a third before the break to put the home crowd in dreamland.

Johnny Russell added a fourth nine minutes into the second-half before Bryson completed his treble from the penalty spot.

NOTTINGHAM FOREST 2
DERBY COUNTY 3
4 FEBRUARY 2009

New Derby boss Nigel Clough headed back to the ground where he had enjoyed so much success as a player and masterminded a memorable FA Cup victory for the Rams.

After the two sides had played out a 1-1 draw in the initial fourth round tie at Pride Park, it was off to the City Ground on Wednesday 4 February 2009 for this eagerly awaited replay.

Forest made home advantage count and were two up inside 15 minutes, but when Rob Hulse pulled a goal back midway through the first half, the tie was back in the balance.

Second-half goals from Paul Green and Kris Commons completed the comeback and handed the Rams a glamour fifth round tie at home to Manchester United.

DERBY COUNTY 3
NOTTINGHAM FOREST 0
11 DECEMBER 2004

The Rams turned on the style to register a comprehensive victory over their bitter rivals on 11 December 2004.

Derby were making strides under the management of George Burley ahead of this meeting, which happened to be the first match between the two clubs since the death of Brian Clough.

To the delight of the home fans, Derby got the game off to the best possible of starts when Tommy Smith first them in front after just four minutes.

Polish striker Grzegorz Rasiak then became the Rams two-goal hero with a header after 75 minutes and neat finish in the 89th to wrap up a memorable home win.

The goals of striker Bobby Davison helped Derby County enjoy a magnificent two-season rise from the Third to First Division in the mid-1980s.

After the Rams had suffered relegation to the Third Division in 1984, the club appointed Arthur Cox as manager and it was he who paired Davison and Phil Gee together to spearhead back-to-back promotions at the Baseball Ground as Derby County returned to the big time.

Davison joined the Rams in 1982 from Halifax Town and his performances and goals soon made him a popular character with the Derby fans. He was top scorer with 22 goals (19 in the league) in 1986/87 as Cox's men won the Second Division title for the fourth time in the club's history.

BORN:

ROBERT DAVISON
17 JULY 1959
SOUTH SHIELDS

POSITION:

STRIKER

RAMS DEBUT:

DERBY COUNTY 3
ROTHERHAM UNITED 0
DIVISION TWO
4 DECEMBER 1982

TAT ATTACK
BOBBY DAVISON

RAMS APPEARANCES:

APPEARANCES	LEAGUE	FA CUP	LEAGUE CUP	OTHERS
249	216	11	18	4

RAMS GOALS:

GOALS	LEAGUE	FA CUP	LEAGUE CUP	OTHERS
106	91	7	6	2

PLAYER OF THE SEASON:

1984/85

SCOTT CARSON

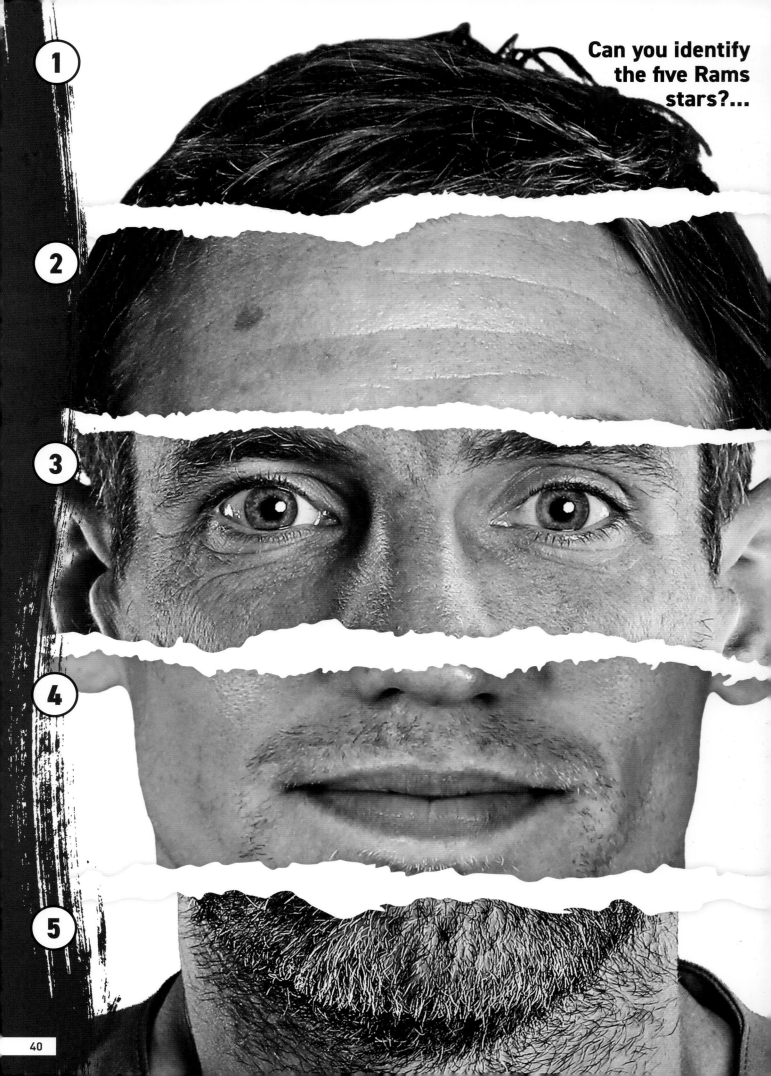

Can you identify the five Rams stars?...

6

7

8

WHO ARE YER?

ANSWERS ON PAGE 62

FLORIAN JOZEFZOON

THE FLIP FLAP

Practise! Practise! Practise!

1. Start by getting familiar with the leg movement.

Push the ball with the outside of your foot.

TIP: Try performing the movement while hopping

TIP: Practise performing the movement while moving forwards and backwards

2. Then move your foot around the ball and bring it back in towards your body.

AKA 'the Elastico'

This move is used by many players and was made famous first by Rivelino in the 1970s and more recently by Ronaldinho. It is a simple technique and done right, really works! The idea behind it is to unbalance your defender by moving the ball one way before using some tricky footwork to move off in another direction!

3. Once you're familiar with the movement, try it while dribbling the ball forward.

TIP: Work on perfecting the technique, then when you're ready you can start moving the ball further away from your body to really confuse your defender

4. Push the ball with the outside of your foot, away from your body. As your defender moves in the direction of the ball...

5. ...Move your foot around the ball, drag it back across your body and move off in the other direction.

43

We take a look at three great Rams games from last season...

◀◀ REWIND

DERBY COUNTY 2 FOREST 0

16 OCTOBER 2017

Matej Vydra scored after just 24 seconds as Derby County beat Nottingham Forest in the East Midlands derby at Pride Park last season.

In what was the 100th domestic meeting between the two great rivals, Vydra caught the Forest defence napping as he sent a smart shot past visiting 'keeper Jordan Smith to give the Rams a dream start.

David Nugent added the second goal to secure the win five minutes into the second half as the Rams ended a run of five Championship games without a victory and moved themselves above Forest in the Championship table.

PRESTON NORTH END 0 DERBY COUNTY 1

2 APRIL 2018

The Rams secured a vital three points against fellow Play-Offs hopefuls Preston North End with a hard-fought 1-0 win at Deepdale on Easter Monday.

After suffering a shock 4-1 defeat at home to struggling Sunderland on Good Friday, this victory could not have come at a better and against a better opponent.

The fact that North End finished the season just two points, and one place, shy of the Rams, demonstrated the importance of this victory. All three points were secured thanks to a Tom Lawrence's goal seven minutes into the second half.

DERBY COUNTY 4 BARNSLEY 1

6 MAY 2018

Derby County rounded off their 2017/18 Sky Bet Championship campaign with an emphatic 4-1 victory over Barnsley, as the Rams booked their place in the end-of-season Play-Offs.

Striker Cameron Jerome opened the scoring after just 14 minutes against the relegation threatened Tykes. The game remained in the balance until a blistering spell of football from the home side in the second half saw them score three goals in a 16-minute period to lead 4-0.

Matej Vydra, Dave Nugent and Tom Lawrence were the players to join Jerome on the score-sheet as Derby warmed-up for the Play-Offs in style. The Tykes managed a late consolation strike, but it was not enough to prevent the Oakwell club from the drop.

1 Who scored Derby County's first League goal last season?

ANSWER

ANSWER

2 What was the score when the Rams knocked Grimsby Town out of the League Cup?

3 Who top-scored last season with 21 league goals?

ANSWER

4 Last season, Derby's highest goalscoring performance was against which team and what was the score?

ANSWER

5 How many clean sheets did the Rams keep in the League in 2017/18?

ANSWER

ANSWER

6 Which player made the most League appearances in 2017/18 with 46?

2017/18 END OF TERM EXAM

How much did you learn about the Rams' last campaign?

7

Who was Derby County's first win of the 2017/18 season against?

ANSWER

8

ANSWER

Which Rams player received the most yellow cards in the League last season?

9 Who scored the goals when the Rams beat Nottingham Forest 2-0 at Pride Park

ANSWER

10

How many goals did Derby County score in the League last season?

ANSWER

FAST FORWARD>>

Three games to look forward to in 2019...

MIDDLESBROUGH
HOME · 1 JANUARY 2019

The Rams begin the New Year with a Pride Park meeting against promotion hopefuls Boro.

Just like Derby, Tony Pulis' Boro fell at the Play-Off semi-final stage last season and will be striving to achieve automatic promotion this season. After finishing fifth in the Championship last season, Boro saw their hopes of an immediate return to the Premier League dashed when they narrowly lost to Aston Villa in the Play-Offs.

When the two clubs met last season, Matej Vydra was the Rams' hat-trick hero in an impressive 3-0 win at the Riverside. However, Vydra and his teammates were unable to complete a league double over Boro who ran out 2-1 winners in the return fixture at Pride Park in April 2018.

NOTTINGHAM FOREST
AWAY · 23 FEBRUARY 2019

There are just ten weeks separating the two East Midlands derby matches this season.

With Pride Park set to host the first Derby/Forest clash on December 15, the two clubs will do it all again at the City Ground on 23 February 2019.

The Rams took local bragging rights last season after goals from Matej Vydra and David Nugent gave Derby a 2-0 home win. That success was followed by a goalless draw at the City Ground later in the season as the Rams closed in on a Play-Off place. Derby fans will be hopeful that new manager Frank Lampard can get his troops fired up to maintain local pride this season.

WEST BROMWICH ALBION
HOME · 5 MAY 2019

Derby complete their gruelling 46-game Sky Bet Championship campaign with a mouth-watering final day fixture at home to West Bromwich Albion.

Relegated from the Premier League last season, the Baggies will be keen to engineer a swift return to the top-flight under the management of former Hawthorns favourite Darren Moore. Albion have retained a number of their Premier League stars and will be well fancied for promotion.

Following the summer arrival of Frank Lampard, optimism is high for a successful season here at Pride Park, therefore this fixture really could have an awful lot resting on it for both teams.

PREDICTION FOR PREMIER LEAGUE WINNERS:

Liverpool

YOUR PREDICTION:

PREDICTION FOR CHAMPIONSHIP WINNERS:

Derby County

YOUR PREDICTION:

PREDICTION FOR FA CUP WINNERS:

Arsenal

YOUR PREDICTION:

PREDICTION FOR PREMIER LEAGUE RUNNERS-UP:

Manchester City

YOUR PREDICTION:

PREDICTION FOR CHAMPIONSHIP RUNNERS-UP:

Norwich City

YOUR PREDICTION:

2018/19 PREDICTIONS

Here are our predictions for the 2018/19 season...

What do you think will happen?

PREDICTION FOR PREMIER LEAGUE TOP SCORER:

Harry Kane

YOUR PREDICTION:

PREDICTION FOR CHAMPIONSHIP TOP SCORER:

Tom Lawrence

YOUR PREDICTION:

PREDICTION FOR LEAGUE CUP WINNERS:

Burnley

YOUR PREDICTION:

#BOY'S GOT SKILLS
THE OKOCHA STEP OVER

Jay-Jay Okocha was one of the best tricksters the Premier League has ever seen. He was effortless in getting past his opponents and here we take a look at how to perform one of his most famous moves...

1. While running...

...roll the ball with the inside of your right foot across your body to the left.

TIP:
Roll the ball far enough out across your body so it doesn't get stuck under your feet.

2. Fake like you're going to hit it with your left foot...

Tip:
Practise until you can master the move off both feet!

3. ...but step over it instead!

4. While you're performing the step over...

...do a quick body feint to the right to help throw off your opponent.

5. Continue going left...

...leaving your opponent wondering what just happened!

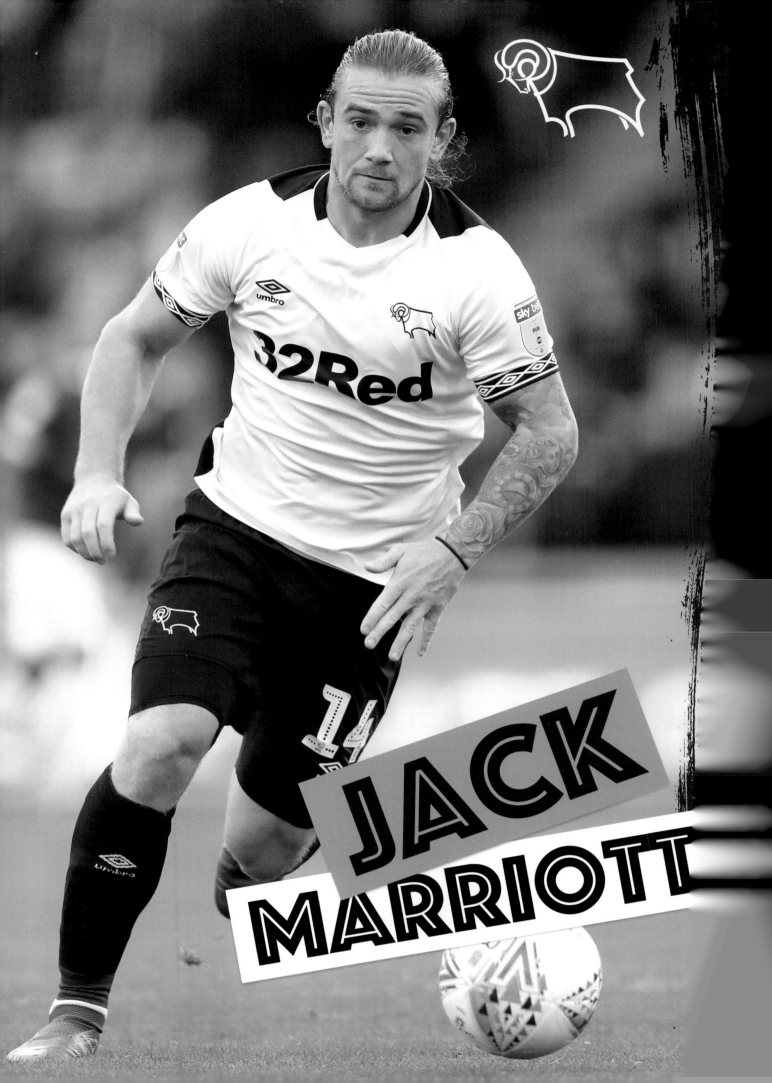

JACK MARRIOTT

GREAT GAFFERS

The appointment of Frank Lampard as the Rams' new boss in the summer certainly sparked a feel-good factor around Pride Park. As Lampard begins his managerial career here at Derby, he follows in the footsteps of some truly great managers who have taken charge of the Rams. Here we look back on the success of four past Derby bosses.

BRIAN CLOUGH

In 1967, Brian Clough took over at the Baseball Ground and led the Rams to their greatest glory. Having clinched the influential signing of Dave Mackay, Derby were promoted to the top flight in 1969 as Second Division Champions.

In 1971/72, Clough's side were crowned First Division champions. Though Derby did not retain their title the following season, they did reach the semi-finals of the European Cup, where they lost to Juventus. Such was the impact that Clough and his assistant Peter Taylor had on the on the club, that a bronze statue of the pair was erected outside Pride Park in commemoration of their legacy. Clough later enjoyed managerial success with East Midlands rivals Nottingham Forest and remains a true legend at both clubs.

ARTHUR COX

Arthur Cox stepped into the manager's chair at Derby County in 1984, just after the club had suffered relegation to the Third Division. Cox guided the Rams to promotion two years later in the 1985/86 campaign.

The following season, 1986/87, saw the Rams win the Second Division title to end a seven-year exile from the First Division. In October 1988, Cox paid a then club record £1M to Oxford United for striker Dean Saunders who soon established himself as one of the best strikers in the First Division. As Rams' boss, Cox also signed defender Mark Wright from Southampton and created a team that emerged as surprise title contenders in the 1988/89 season. His other notable acquisitions included England goalkeeper Peter Shilton.

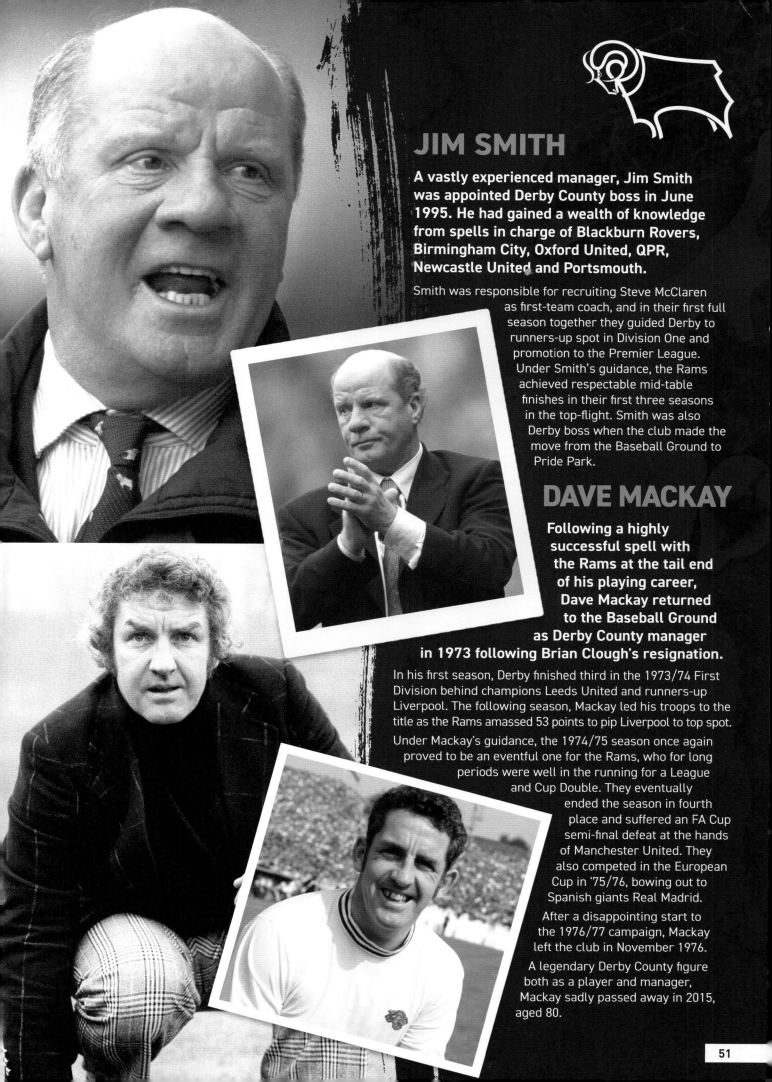

JIM SMITH

A vastly experienced manager, Jim Smith was appointed Derby County boss in June 1995. He had gained a wealth of knowledge from spells in charge of Blackburn Rovers, Birmingham City, Oxford United, QPR, Newcastle United and Portsmouth.

Smith was responsible for recruiting Steve McClaren as first-team coach, and in their first full season together they guided Derby to runners-up spot in Division One and promotion to the Premier League. Under Smith's guidance, the Rams achieved respectable mid-table finishes in their first three seasons in the top-flight. Smith was also Derby boss when the club made the move from the Baseball Ground to Pride Park.

DAVE MACKAY

Following a highly successful spell with the Rams at the tail end of his playing career, Dave Mackay returned to the Baseball Ground as Derby County manager in 1973 following Brian Clough's resignation.

In his first season, Derby finished third in the 1973/74 First Division behind champions Leeds United and runners-up Liverpool. The following season, Mackay led his troops to the title as the Rams amassed 53 points to pip Liverpool to top spot.

Under Mackay's guidance, the 1974/75 season once again proved to be an eventful one for the Rams, who for long periods were well in the running for a League and Cup Double. They eventually ended the season in fourth place and suffered an FA Cup semi-final defeat at the hands of Manchester United. They also competed in the European Cup in '75/76, bowing out to Spanish giants Real Madrid.

After a disappointing start to the 1976/77 campaign, Mackay left the club in November 1976.

A legendary Derby County figure both as a player and manager, Mackay sadly passed away in 2015, aged 80.

FIRST ELEVEN

Choose your all-time First Eleven, put their names and numbers on the back of the shirts, then colour them in!

SPOT THE BALL

The ball is missing from this photo, where should it be?

WHAT BALL?

Can you figure out which is the real ball in this photo?

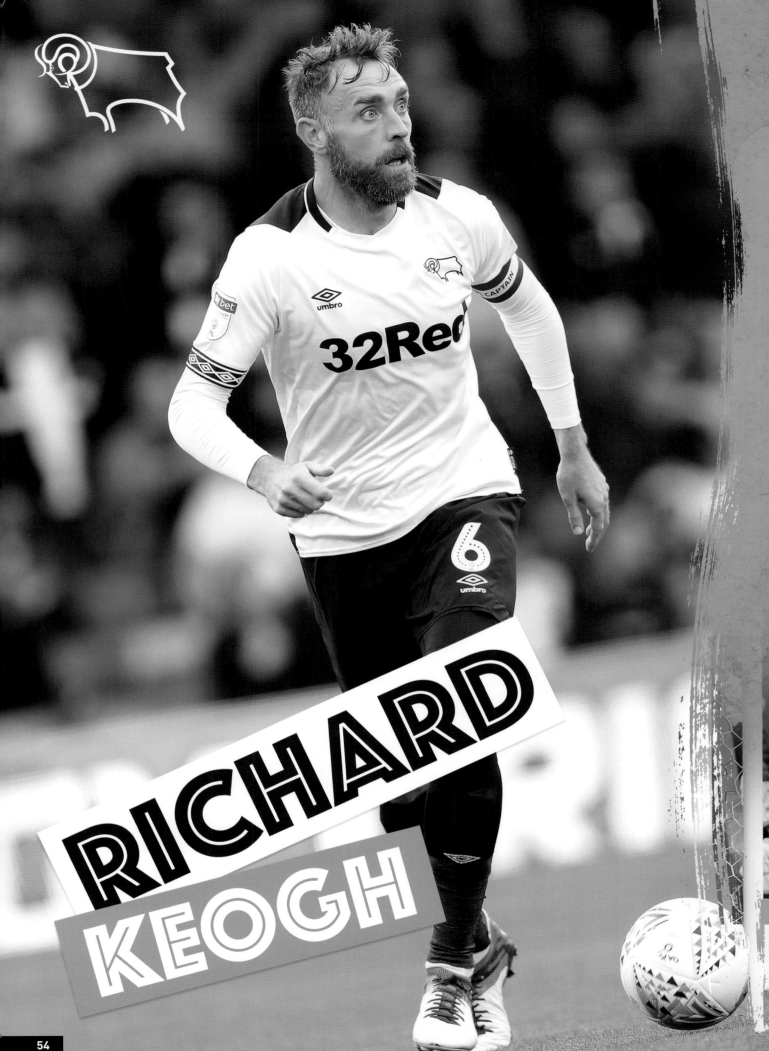

RICHARD
KEOGH

Magic MOMENT 56'

LOCAL *Pride*

FIXTURE: npower Championship

DATE: Sunday 30 September 2012

SCORE: Nottingham Forest 0 Derby County 1

VENUE: City Ground

ATTENDANCE: 28,707

The Rams took the local bragging rights with a hard-fought 1-0 win away to arch-rivals Nottingham Forest in September 2012.

In what was a fiery affair from the off, Derby sealed victory in this East Midlands derby match thanks to Craig Bryson's 56th minute goal at the City Ground.

The home side had been reduced to ten men at the start of the second-half after Dexter Blackstock had seen red for an elbow on Richard Keogh.

Derby then made their numerical advantage count when a lovely move down the right involving John Brayford, Will Hughes and Paul Coutts ended with the latter squaring an enticing centre which Bryson slotted home. The goal gave the Rams a third consecutive victory over Forest.

HERO HUNT

Here is a list of 20 Rams heroes. All but one of their surnames are hidden in the grid, can you work out who is missing?

```
N N C G N O B J S D K I O K Y I E B B T P H
M D U M J E Y I J U Y F O S N A B R U D I T
E F W G E M M I L L H A C N I G I J V J G C
A H O H B H U L D X Q U Z Y N A H E T R K E
K A L F T C J T E O R K C W D E A I S D L A
N I A V G Y B S P R L V S J C F X T N A M S
N T F I B G S M K C R E B T B T Z W H T M R
C P H Z O A T R S U W L O A I O G S H Y O H
J C S Q R B L O O M E R Y S P M T O M L F N
U E Y D B O M B S F O E P U F D A U Q I E W
T L S A X U A A A I F Q I W N R P C G V Q E
O X N W W L N T H D E D G A T I N U B R L B
D E K Z Q T S E E C R T L H O H S F V W X S
D V C U Y O G W Y R M R J O M K R H G K Y T
V O N P T N R R S U A U I B J Z T N D K Z E
P S A B T R M A B F S N F N Y D J G N E P R
O A G U M B V P C L G X I R W A I S U H O S
B G N N I D C A M O E T K O V N M B C H E D
S E A U S T M Q U H N A I E F R T A X G I A
R Y L H V H Y C A Z R C X G P E M S S U Q M
W F G C E A T R M A B S F L H V E G R O E G
I S P I L J E N W I K E D P R O S I U L I O
A L C Q O Y D U V Z N F J O A G L L J C Q D
U V W X D J O H N S O N H A B C K T O R G F
K O L J T A Z K D U L V C J M M K J L H U A
```

Steve **Bloomer**	Frank **Fielding**	Alan **Hinton**	Ted **McMinn**
Colin **Boulton**	Mick **Forsyth**	Seth **Johnson**	David **Nish**
Brian **Clough**	Archie **Gemmill**	David **Langan**	Igor **Stimac**
Alan **Durban**	Charlie **George**	Roy **MacFarland**	Colin **Todd**
Stefano **Eranio**	Kevin **Hector**	John **McGovern**	Ron **Webster**

ANSWERS ON PAGE 62

SHIRT SHUFFLE

1 RLVOELPOI

2 ALUMHF

3 FEEHFLDIS NIEUDT

4 RNGBIHMMIA TIYC

5 TEWS AMH DUTNIE

6 YCTSLRA LAPEAC

Here are the away shirts of twelve Premier League and Championship clubs, but their team names have been jumbled up!

Can you figure out who's who?

7 OONEUMTBRUH

8 NQESEU RKAP GRARNES

9 KOETS TCIY

10 WESATNELC TUNEDI

11 ROTPENS HRTNO NDE

12 NATOS LAVIL

Striker Steve Howard only spent 18 months at Pride Park, but became a real fans' favourite during the 2006/07 season as his goals inspired the club to Premier League promotion.

Derby fought off interest from a host of other clubs to secure Howard's services for a £1M fee in the summer of 2006.

The powerful frontman ended the 2006/07 season as top goalscorer with 19 goals, 16 of which came in the Championship.

He is fondly remembered for his vital brace in the first leg of the epic Play-Off semi-final meeting with Southampton. He played in the Play-Off final victory over West Bromwich Albion at Wembley and represented the Rams in the Premier League.

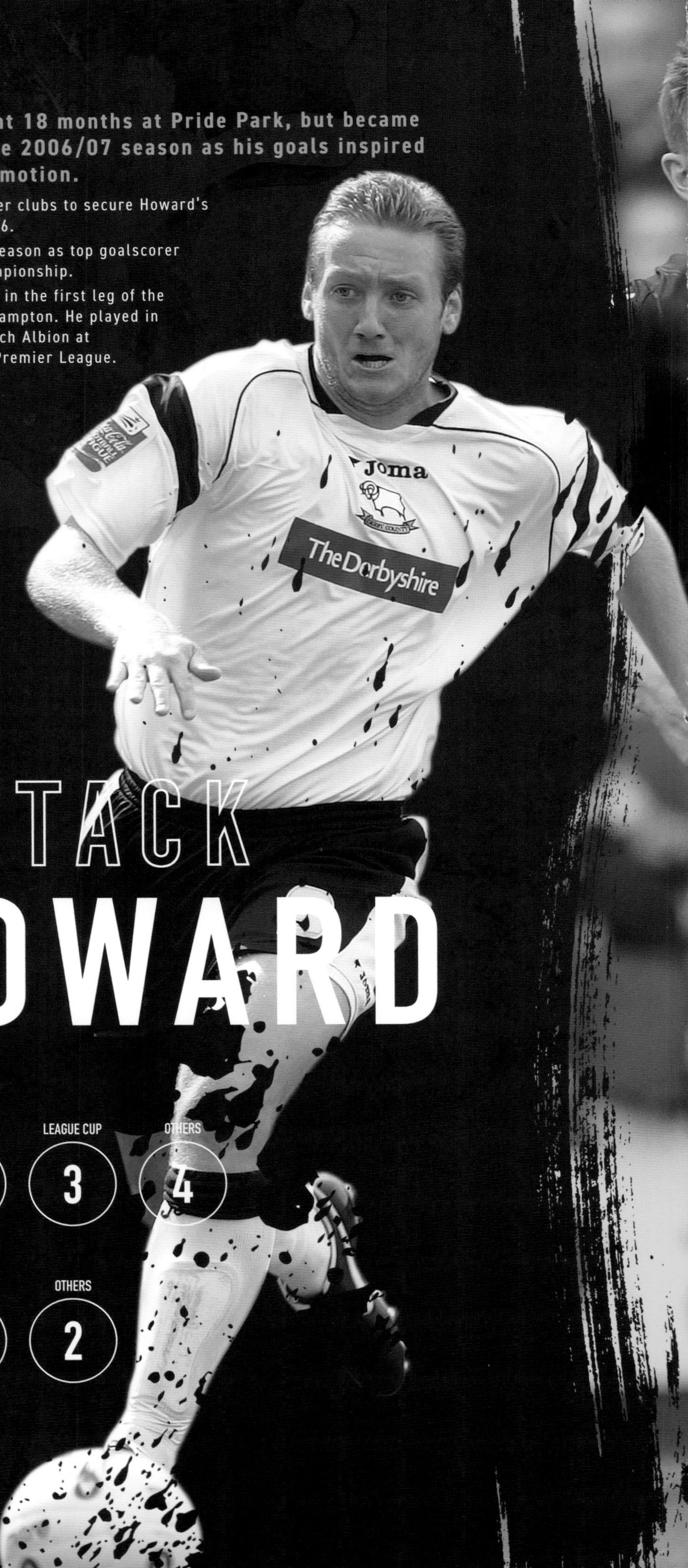

BORN:

STEVEN JOHN HOWARD
10 MAY 1976
DURHAM

POSITION:

STRIKER

RAMS DEBUT:

DERBY COUNTY 2–2 SOUTHAMPTON
CHAMPIONSHIP
6 AUGUST 2006

STAT ATTACK
STEVE HOWARD

RAMS APPEARANCES:

APPEARANCES	LEAGUE	FA CUP	LEAGUE CUP	OTHERS
73	63	3	3	4

RAMS GOALS:

GOALS	LEAGUE	LEAGUE CUP	OTHERS
20	17	1	2

PLAYER OF THE SEASON:

2006/07

MARTYN
WAGHORN

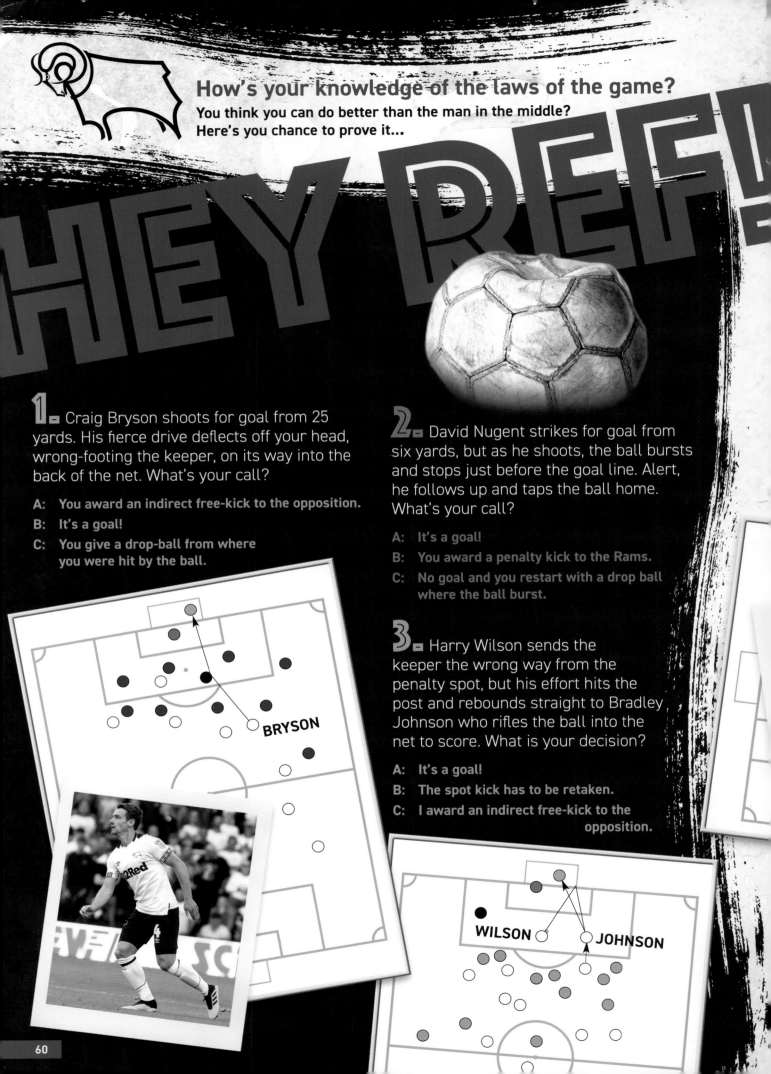

How's your knowledge of the laws of the game?

You think you can do better than the man in the middle?
Here's you chance to prove it...

HEY REF!

1. Craig Bryson shoots for goal from 25 yards. His fierce drive deflects off your head, wrong-footing the keeper, on its way into the back of the net. What's your call?

A: You award an indirect free-kick to the opposition.

B: It's a goal!

C: You give a drop-ball from where you were hit by the ball.

2. David Nugent strikes for goal from six yards, but as he shoots, the ball bursts and stops just before the goal line. Alert, he follows up and taps the ball home. What's your call?

A: It's a goal!

B: You award a penalty kick to the Rams.

C: No goal and you restart with a drop ball where the ball burst.

3. Harry Wilson sends the keeper the wrong way from the penalty spot, but his effort hits the post and rebounds straight to Bradley Johnson who rifles the ball into the net to score. What is your decision?

A: It's a goal!

B: The spot kick has to be retaken.

C: I award an indirect free-kick to the opposition.

BRYSON

WILSON   JOHNSON

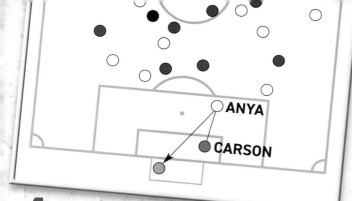

4. Scott Carson attempts to take a quick goal kick, but to his horror, it hits Ikechi Anya who is still in the penalty area and the ball deflects into his own net. What's your call?

A: It's a goal!
B: A corner kick to the opposing team
C: The Goal kick has to be retaken.

5. Standing in his own penalty area, Scott Carson catches the ball directly from teammate Richard Keogh's throw-in. What's your decision?

A: Everything's fine. Play on.
B: You award the opposing team an indirect free-kick.
C: A yellow card for Carson and a penalty for the opposing team.

6. You have decided Mason Mount's spot kick must be re-taken after an infringement by the keeper. This time Tom Lawrence steps forward to take the kick. Is that allowed?

A: No, I award an indirect free kick to the opposition.
B: Yes, any Rams player can re-take the penalty.
C: No, the player who took the initial spot kick, Mason Mount, must retake the kick.

7. You award a drop ball. As you drop the ball, Tom Lawrence and the opposing player both kick the ball at the same time before it hits the turf. What's your ruling?

A: You show a yellow card to both players for ungentlemanly conduct.
B: You drop the ball again.
C: Play on.

8. Tom Lawrence is on the scoresheet again, tapping in from only three yards out. When he scores, he is slightly ahead of the last defender, but in line with the goalkeeper. What is your decision?

A: Goal. in line with the keeper is not offside.
B: Goal disallowed. Lawrence is offside. To be onside, he must be in line with the second last opponent or the ball.
C: Goal. A player can't be offside inside the six-yard box.

9. Craig Bryson takes a long throw in aiming for the head of David Nugent. No-one makes contact with the ball and it bounces into the net direct from Bryson's throw. What's your call, ref?

A: Goal. Providing there was an attempt to play the ball.
B: Goal. As long as the throw-in was taken correctly.
C: No Goal. A goal can never be scored direct from a throw in.

ANSWERS

PAGE 26 · FAN'TASTIC

Raheem Sterling, Ben Alnwick, Harry Maguire, Jordan Henderson and Harry Kane.

PAGE 34 · GUESS THE CLUB

1. Ajax. 2. Paris Saint-Germain. 3. Bayern Munich.
4. Sporting Lisbon. 5. Real Madrid. 6. Arsenal. 7. Celtic.
8. Juventus. 9. Barcelona. 10. Club Brugge.

PAGE 40 · WHO ARE YER?

1. Richard Keogh. 2. Jack Marriott. 3. Craig Bryson.
4. Martyn Waghorn. 5. Scott Carson. 6. Joe Ledley.
7. Jayden Bogle. 8. Martyn Waghorn.

PAGE 44 · 2018/19 END OF TERM EXAM

1. Bradley Johnson. 2. 1-0. 3. Matej Vydra. 4. 5-0 v Hull City.
5. 19. 6. Scott Carson 7. Preston North End. 8. Bradley Johnson, 10.
9. Matej Vydra and David Nugent. 10. 69.

PAGE 53 · SPOT THE BALL

PAGE 53 · WHAT BALL?

Ball F.

PAGE 56 · HERO HUNT

Frank Fielding.

PAGE 57 · SHIRT SHUFFLE

1. Liverpool. 2. Fulham. 3. Sheffield United. 4. Birmingham City.
5. West Ham United. 6. Crystal Palace. 7. Bournemouth.
8. Queens Park Rangers. 9. Stoke City. 10. Newcastle United.
11. Preston North End. 12. Aston Villa

PAGE 60 · ASK THE REF

1. B. 2. C. 3. A. 4. C. 5. B. 6. B. 7. B. 8. B. 9. C.